AF870997

I Purr, *Therefore* I Am

INNER MONOLOGUES OF THE DOMESTICATED

I Purr, *Therefore* I Am

Inner Monologues of the Domesticated

CHARLOTTE JEAN

the collective book studio

As you might
have suspected,
Mr. Goldfish,
I have terrible
news for you.

Excuse me, I have an idea. You chase the mice and I sit around all day watching Netflix.

You have permission
to detain my owner.

Hey, where's
the toy with
the feather-thingy?

Does this come in mouse flavor?

I see that you got rid of my scratching post without consulting me.

I bring sad tidings concerning the canary.

This generic kibble
isn't cutting it.

Oh, we're definitely smarter than the humans. I mean, do you go to a job you hate five days a week?

Change this please.
Right after you get
my dinner.

Don't even
talk to me.
Not now.
Not ever.

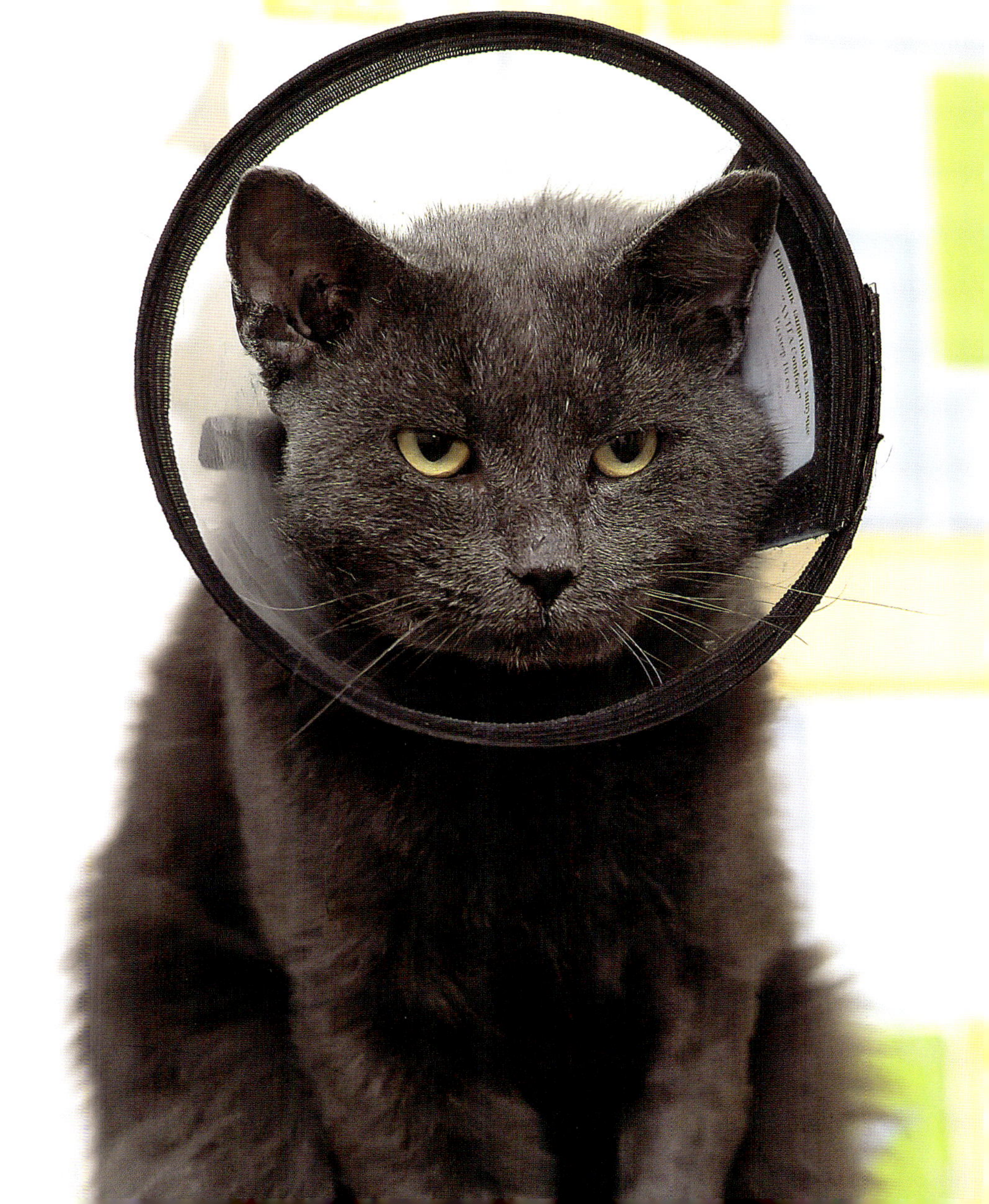

Did she just say
"No more cat treats"?

Call the fire department!

My owner seems to think that she is an actual witch. Who's going to tell her she needs a black cat?

Who let that in?

“Bath time” stinks.

Now I just need the
world's dumbest bird
to fly in here.

I realize that you've never seen anything quite as amazing as me before, but you'll just have to get used to it.

For the last time,
I am not a "kitty cat."
I am a petite tiger.

The human still looks mad that I attacked her leg.

Our relationship really started to go downhill when she began learning this ghastly instrument.

No, it's *not* the wet food that is making me gain weight. It's the fact that I hardly ever move.

How about you
pick *me* up instead of
this dusty old book?

This is a little after the fact, but just checking that it's ok to poop in that pot with the tomato plant out back?

I certainly do not want to go on a trip with you. This is just super cozy.

Pretty sure I can pin this on the dog.

Well, hello handsome.

How do I keep getting myself into these predicaments?

I guess I should wake up from this nap so I can get ready for bed.

Sorry, but I can recognize farmed salmon a mile away.

Was it you playing
the loud music
half the night?

Worship me as
your ancestors did.

I know it seems ridiculous, but if you pet me one more time I will attack you.

Look, human,
your two favorite
things in one place.

I am not sure if this
is a sign of affection
or if he is preparing
to eat my head.

This might sound weird, but if you poo in a box at my house, a hairless ape with a tiny plastic shovel will come take it away.

I love you, big orange ball in the sky.

It's pretty early in
the morning . . .
Probably time to go
sleep on the human's
face for a while.

Oh, I love when they bring out the giant cat toy once a year.

Change the
channel already!

Has that tail-pulling kid left yet?

What?
The dog ran away?
Best news ever!

That's it.
Put your back into it.

I resent that
"old barn cat"
remark.

Why can't he just be courteous and use his tongue to clean me?

I’m on the fence
about it. Literally.

I disagree with
the man-ape.
You look terrible
in those jeans.

Purrfect. Now please try not to move.

Let's agree that today
was the last vet visit
for a while.

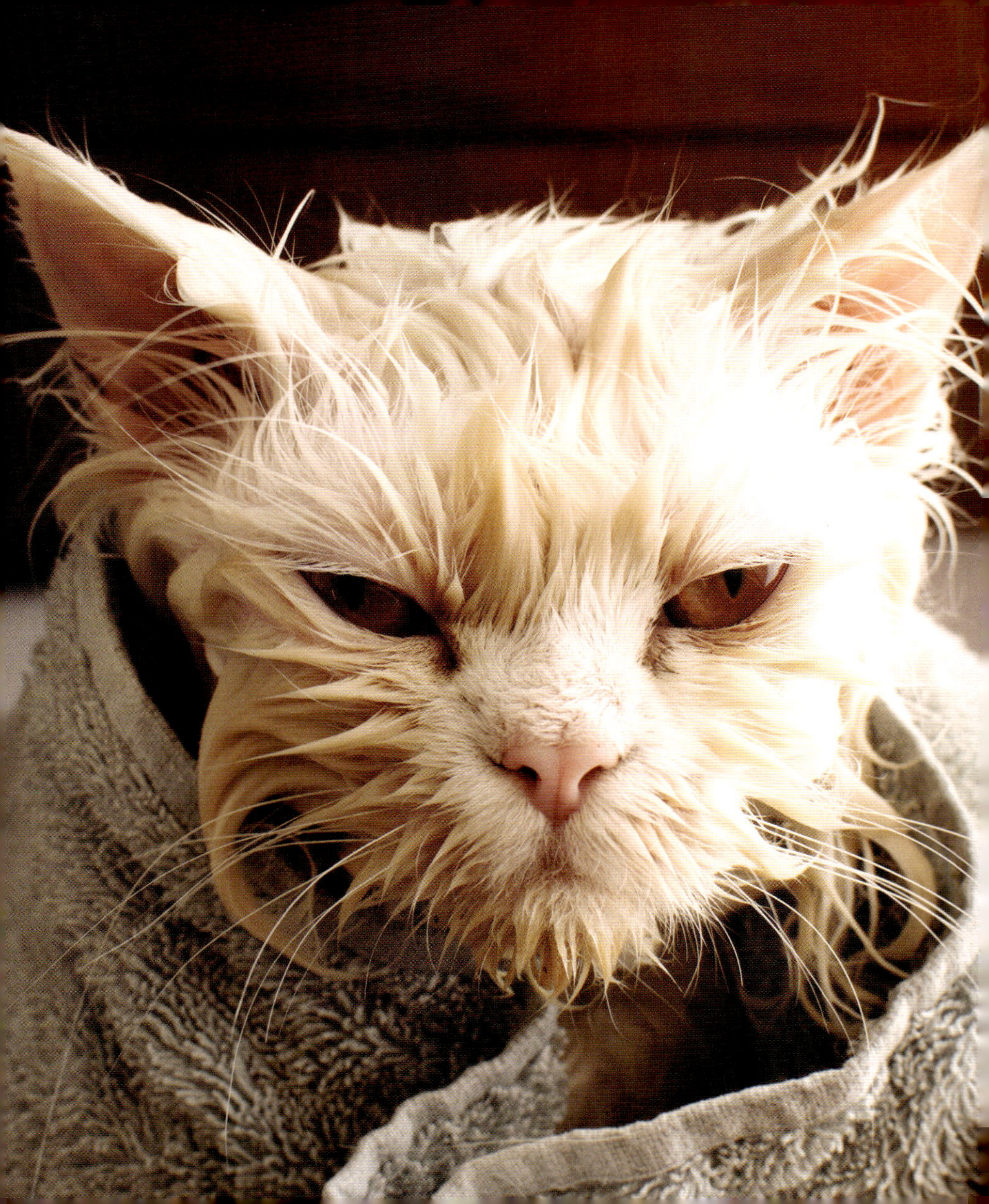

How about we keep the whole "me falling in the pool" story just between us?

That catnip stuff
is great!

Can you get the two-ply roll next time? It has a better "paw feel".

Even though he does
my every bidding,
I'm still growing
weary of the human's
foolish behavior.

Oh, I can still taste that delicious mouse.

That's the last time
I stay up so late
yowling in the alley
with the guys.

Can you believe this amazing sight? You may also want to check out the building behind me.

I will never forgive you for taking the bird away from me.

Frankly, I find your name change for me from "Catniss" to "Fatniss" both childish and rude.

If the she-ape isn't back with the milk soon, I say we pee on her bed.

I'll play with you, Mr. Ball, but only if you promise not to get stuck under the couch again.

Oh, were these yours?

Please excuse me, but I'm about to make a spectacle of myself with this ball of yarn.

That's the spot!

I think I'll head home, let the humans fuss and fawn all over me, and then leave the moment that I'm fuflilled.

Where's the handle on this thing?